D0984154

FISHING THE FLATS

KRISTI LEW

rosen publishing's
rosen central

New York

Published in 2014 by The Rosen Publishing Group, Inc.
29 East 21st Street, New York, NY 10010

Copyright © 2014 by The Rosen Publishing Group, Inc.

First Edition

All rights reserved. No part of this book may be reproduced in any form without permission in writing from the publisher, except by a reviewer.

Library of Congress Cataloging-in-Publication Data

Lew, Kristi.
Fishing the flats/Kristi Lew.
    pages cm.—(Fishing: tips & techniques)
Includes bibliographical references and index.
ISBN 978-1-4488-9487-1 (library binding)—ISBN 978-1-4488-9504-5 (pbk.)—
ISBN 978-1-4488-9505-2 (6-pack)
1. Saltwater fishing—Juvenile literature. I. Title.
SH457.3.L49 2014
799.16—dc23

2012043298

Manufactured in the United States of America

CPSIA Compliance Information: Batch #S13YA: For further information, contact Rosen Publishing, New York, New York, at 1-800-237-9932.

CONTENTS

*A*ccording to the 2011 national survey conducted by the U.S. Fish and Wildlife Service (FWS), more than thirty-three million people tossed fishing lines into the water that year. Probably that was because fishing can be a whole lot of fun! This challenging hobby allows participants the opportunity to play in the beautiful outdoors, engage in the thrill of the hunt, revel in the satisfaction of skills well learned, and take pride in the ability to put food on the table. Many life-long friendships, unforgettable memories, and unlimited adventure can occur in the quest for the perfect fishing hole.

In general, when anglers think of flats, they think of shallow water. The term "shallow" is relative, however. Along the coast of the Gulf of Mexico or in a relatively shallow lake, a flat may be anywhere from 8 inches (20 centimeters) to 10 feet (3 meters) deep. In other, deeper lakes and bodies of water, a flat could be 15 feet (4.6 m) deep or more. The main feature that defines a flat is a bottom that slopes gently to the shore with very few, if any, steep drop-offs. In other words, the water depth does not change dramatically over a particular area. In some

Beyond a fishing rod and some bait, fishing the flats requires no additional equipment—not even a boat!

lakes, a flat may be very small. In the Gulf of Mexico, a flat may go on for acres.

Fishing the flats brings with it some unique challenges and opportunities. Anglers fishing these clear, shallow waters must be able to cast with finesse and precision or risk scaring their prey away. But the clear water also allows anglers to easily observe how fish react to the bait, lures, or flies offered to them and adjust their choices accordingly.

Opportunities for flats fishing abound along the Eastern seaboard from the Florida Keys to Cape Cod and many areas in between. Anglers may fish the flats from specially equipped boats or by simply wading into the shallow water.

Some of the most favored destinations for flats fishing are the west coast of Florida and the Florida Keys. Florida anglers are likely to encounter tarpon, bonefish, snook, red drum (also called redfish), barracuda, permit, and cobia. Flats anglers fishing in freshwater may encounter bass, striped bass, or other fish species. Whether you are fishing for bass on the flats of a lake near your home or for bonefish on the flats of Florida, this sport can be challenging, relaxing, and a great deal of fun. Let the journey begin!

CHAPTER 1

SAFETY AND THE SAVVY ANGLER

Although fishing can be a fun, relaxing activity, there are a few matters that anglers need to keep in mind before tossing their lines in the water. One of the first things that savvy anglers learn is that it is not safe to be around the water alone. Besides, it is much more fun to go fishing with friends or family. If you decide to go fishing with a group of friends, make sure an adult knows where you have gone. If your family is planning to go out on a boat, make sure someone onshore knows where you are going and when you expect to come back. This information is called a float plan. Other valuable information to include in your float plan are a description of your boat, the names of family members and friends that will be onboard, and what type of safety equipment you have with you. Instruct the person you are leaving the float plan with to contact the Coast Guard or other local

Thunderstorms can build quickly over the water. Keep an eye on the clouds while you are fishing and be prepared to head inland if a storm gets too close.

maritime authority if you don't return in a reasonable amount of time after you said that you would.

The weather can change quickly on the water. Always check the weather forecast before you go out. But it is also important to remember to keep an eye on the sky while you fish. Clouds that rise high into the air and flatten out at their tops in an anvil shape are sure signs that a thunderstorm is brewing. When you see this cloud formation happening, it is time to pack up your gear and get ready to head home. If you hear thunder, it is definitely time to go inside. According to the National Oceanic and Atmospheric Administration (NOAA), humans can hear thunder about 10 miles (16.1 kilometers) away from its source, and lightning can strike up to 10 miles (16.1 km) away from a thunderstorm. That means if you can hear thunder, you are within the strike zone. Sadly, lightning strikes claim the lives of several dozen people around the United States every year.

Smart anglers also wear a personal flotation device (PFD) any time they are around the water. PFDs are sometimes called life jackets or life vests, with good reason—wearing one could save your life. Even the most careful angler can get caught by surprise and fall off the deck of a boat or the side of a dock. Even the strongest swimmers can get caught in rip currents and become so tired that they cannot swim safely back to shore. PFDs help keep you afloat even when you are tired or have hit your head. Most PFDs are brightly colored and adorned with some sort of reflective tape, which makes it easier to find you in the water. If a knock to the head renders you unconscious, having a life vest on may very well save your life. In some situations, wearing a PFD is also the law. Federal law requires that all people age twelve and younger wear a PFD at all times while aboard a boat. Many states have individual PFD regulations, too. Be sure to check the laws in your area before you leave shore.

What to Pack and Wear

Sunscreen is another necessity for a day out on the water. The U.S. Food and Drug Administration (FDA) recommends covering all exposed skin with sunscreen that has a broad-spectrum sun protection factor (SPF) of 15 or higher. To avoid getting sunburned, remember to reapply the sunscreen at least every two hours—more often if you are sweating or in and out of the water. A good pair of polarized sunglasses is an excellent addition to an angler's wardrobe, too. Not only will sunglasses protect your eyes from the sun and rogue hooks, they can also help you see the fish better. A hat with a wide brim can help shade your face and ears as well.

Wearing shoes around docks and boats is also a good idea. An old pair of sneakers can help protect fragile feet from fishing hooks

Having a basic first-aid kit with you can make the difference between a quick repair job and a trip back home.

Leave Nothing But Footprints

Not only do experienced anglers bring what they need to make sure they have a wonderful day on the water; they also plan ahead and prepare to pack out what they pack in. This means anything you take to a fishing site should leave with you, including any trash and food scraps. Trash that is left behind can blow into the water. A plastic shopping bag could be lethal to a sea turtle that mistakes it for its favorite food—jellyfish. Once swallowed, the bag can cause a blockage in the turtle's digestive tract and end up killing the animal. Fishing line can also be particularly dangerous to marine birds and other animals that get tangled in the line. By leaving no trace of your presence, you are doing your part to preserve and maintain the natural surroundings and protect the species that live where you fish.

that might lie on docks or decks. One of the best ways to fish the flats is to wade out into shallow water. While wading, those old tennis shoes also help protect tender toes from sharp oyster beds and other broken debris that might lie on the ocean's bottom. You can also buy waders in many sporting goods shops. These waterproof pants with attached boots not only protect your feet, but also your ankles and legs from spiny or stinging animals, such as stingrays.

Another really good thing to have with you on a fishing trip is a basic first-aid kit. A waterproof pouch that includes disposable gloves, antibiotic ointment, adhesive bandages, scissors, sterile gauze pads,

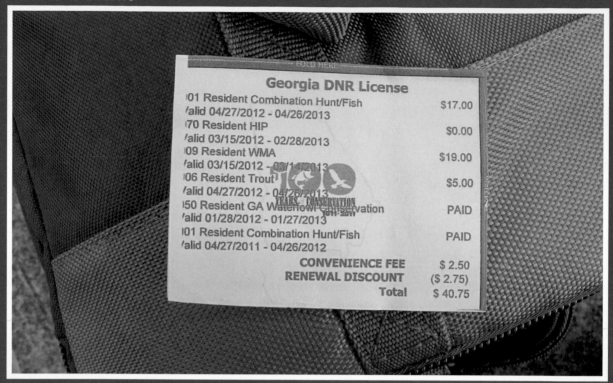

Georgia DNR License

01 Resident Combination Hunt/Fish Valid 04/27/2012 - 04/26/2013	$17.00
70 Resident HIP Valid 03/15/2012 - 02/28/2013	$0.00
09 Resident WMA Valid 03/15/2012 - 03/14/2013	$19.00
06 Resident Trout Valid 04/27/2012 - 04/26/2013	$5.00
50 Resident GA Waterfowl Conservation Valid 01/28/2012 - 01/27/2013	PAID
01 Resident Combination Hunt/Fish Valid 04/27/2011 - 04/26/2012	PAID
CONVENIENCE FEE	$ 2.50
RENEWAL DISCOUNT	($ 2.75)
Total	$ 40.75

Most states require that anglers have a fishing license, such as this one from Georgia. Special permits may be needed to catch specific species, too.

and tape can take care of most cuts and scrapes. Tweezers for taking out splinters, a small bottle of saline solution for use as eyewash, pain reliever, and sting and bite treatments can be useful, too. Depending on where you go fishing, sprays to prevent bugs from biting or stinging can be a necessity.

You need to bring along plenty of water and snacks, too. When you sweat, you lose water that your body needs to function properly, and being out on the water makes people hungry. You would not want to be forced to go home just when the fish are starting to bite because you forgot to pack a snack.

Anglers must comply with the bag limits set by the fishing regulations in their area. All other fish caught should be promptly—and carefully—released.

Fishing Rules and Regulations

Another thing you may need before casting your line is a fishing license. Different states have different rules regarding the age of the angler and which situations require a license. In Florida, for example, anyone who is age sixteen or older needs a license to try to catch fish. You may also need a special permit or tag above and beyond the standard fishing license if you are planning to catch and keep certain fish species, such as snook or tarpon. However, there are exceptions. If you are planning to go out on a charter boat with a valid vessel license, for example, you don't need an individual saltwater fishing license. Plan ahead to make sure you have the proper licenses and other permits you might need for the area you are planning to fish.

Most states also have regulations in place to help protect the fishery. These regulations ensure that there are enough fish for you and others to catch today—and in the future. These rules usually define the number and size of individual fish species you are allowed to take from a certain area during a specific season. For example, Florida's fishing regulations state that any snook caught in the Gulf of Mexico, on Florida's west coast, may not be kept. This catch-and-release policy is in place until at least August 31, 2013, to allow the snook population in the Gulf to recover from the particularly cold winter of 2010. However, the Florida Fish and Wildlife Commission discovered that snook in the Atlantic Ocean were not as severely affected by this cold weather as the ones in the Gulf were. Therefore, the regulations state that snook may be caught on the Atlantic side of Florida between September 1 and December 15 and again from February 1 though May 31. During these open seasons, one snook at least 28 inches (71.1 cm) long but not more than 32 inches (81.3 cm) long may be kept per angler. This one-snook limit is called a bag limit.

There are two common ways of measuring a fish: total length and fork length. Snook are a total-length species. To measure the total length of these fish, the measurement is taken from the most forward point of the head to its compressed tail. Compressing, or squeezing, the fish's tail is often called the pinch-tail criteria. Examples of fork-length species include cobia and permit. These fish are measured from the most forward point of their heads to the junction of the fork in their tails. To keep a cobia, the fish must be at least 33 inches (83.8 cm) long. Because these regulations can change at any time, it's always best to check your state's rules and know the local laws before you pack up your gear and head out on the water.

CHAPTER 2

TACKLE TALK

Fishing the flats does not require complicated or specialized equipment. A fishing rod, a few hooks, something to attract the fish, and your safety gear are all you really need to wade into the shallows and try your hand at catching some fish. The equipment used for fishing is called tackle.

Rods and Reels

The purpose of a fishing rod is to provide support and guidance for the line. Modern fishing poles are made of a variety of materials, including fiberglass, carbon fiber, and bamboo. Fiberglass rods are strong, inexpensive, and require little maintenance. These characteristics make fiberglass rods popular with beginning anglers. Advanced anglers often prefer fishing poles made of carbon fiber. These fishing rods are commonly called graphite rods. Carbon

Many anglers fish the flats with a rod and spinning reel. Lures that imitate the fish's usual prey are useful, too.

fiber is stronger and lighter than fiberglass. However, the material is also more expensive. Anglers who prefer traditional, wooden fishing rods may like the look of a bamboo fishing pole. Nevertheless, bamboo is not as strong as carbon fiber and, therefore, a bamboo rod is easier to break than a graphite one. Bamboo rods also require more maintenance than fiberglass or graphite rods, and they can be quite expensive.

The length of fishing rods varies from 6 to 12 feet (1.83 to 3.66 m). The length is usually marked on the rod or on its packaging. An 8 to 9-foot (2.44 to 2.74-m) rod is a good length for beginners. It's long enough to give a good casting distance, but short enough to help

The action of a rod refers to how much bend the rod has when you cast or hook a fish. The word "speed" is used sometimes for "action," and it refers to how quickly the rod snaps back when it is bent.

develop line control and good casting technique. However, anglers with smaller builds may prefer a shorter rod.

Fishing rods are also marked by the weight of line recommended for that rod. The weight of line refers to its strength and is measured in pounds. One-pound (0.45-kilogram) line is the smallest, thinnest line. Twelve-pound (5.4-kg) line is a larger, heavier line. The weight of the line you choose should roughly match the weight of the fish you are trying to catch. Light line is used for small fish in calm waters. Larger fish caught in the surf, where wind and waves are a factor, will require heavier line. Seven to 9-pound (3.2 to 4.1-kg) line will work if you are fishing for bonefish. However, 10 to 12-pound (4.5 to 5.4-kg) line or even stronger would be needed if you were fishing for tarpon because they are larger, heavier fish.

Rods are often classified by their strength and flexibility. The power of the rod is how strong it is. A rod may be classified as ultra-light, light, medium-light, medium, medium-heavy, heavy, or ultra-heavy. Ultra-light rods are great for catching small fish, but for larger, heavier fish, such as tarpon, a heavier rod is needed. A light-to-medium rod works well for most flats fish species.

The action of a rod is how flexible it is. Flexibility will affect your casting accuracy and distance. Rods can be classified as slow, medium, or fast action. Slow-action rods are very flexible. Because they bend a lot, they work well for catching small fish. Fast-action rods bend just a little bit and are good for casting larger, heavier flies or lures—and for catching larger fish, such as tarpon. The flexibility of a medium-action rod is between that of slow- and fast-action rods. Medium-action rods are a good choice for beginning anglers.

Many anglers fish the flats with a rod and reel. A reel keeps fishing line stored so that it doesn't tangle. It also provides resistance, or drag, which keeps a hooked fish from running away with all of your fishing line. Spinning reels are popular when a lot of casting needs to be done. There are two main types of spinning reels: spin casting and open face. Spin-casting reels are the easiest to use and are often used by beginning anglers, but they have some limitations. Open-face spinning reels are the most popular and capable type of spinning reel. A quality, corrosion-proof reel that can carry at least 200 yards (183 m) of line is useful for fish that make long, hard runs, such as tarpon or bonefish.

Other anglers like the challenge of fishing the flats with a fly fishing rod. In fly fishing, the angler uses a handcrafted lure, called a fly, instead of live baitfish or an artificial lure. The flies are designed to imitate the fish's normal prey. Fly fishing rods are long, thin, and flexible.

To determine the best type of fishing rod for the conditions and type of fish you wish to catch, it may be helpful to consult a local angler or tackle shop professional.

Line, Bait, Lures, and Hooks

Sometimes your line might get tangled on the reel. To fix it, pull enough line off the reel so that you can see the tangle. Taking a tangle out of fishing line is like a puzzle. If you are patient, you can sometimes untangle it. If you can't untangle the line, you'll have to cut it. If you cut tangled line off of your reel, cut it into small pieces and put it in a trash can. If you're at the shore and there is no trash can handy, keep the discarded line until you get back home and throw it away there. Long pieces of tangled fishing line can be dangerous to fish, birds, and small animals that can get caught and trapped in it.

The type of bait or lure you use will depend on what type of fish you are fishing for. Tarpon, for example, like live crabs, shrimp, and baitfish, such as pinfish, blue runners, and greenbacks. Bonefish prefer live shrimp or lures or flies that look and move like live shrimp. Redfish like crab, but they will sometimes go after artificial lures such as spinnerbaits, spoons, and shallow-running crankbaits. Spinnerbaits are lures

This picture shows a large bait bobber, a special hook that is used for fishing in weeds, and a menhaden that is live bait. A bobber is a buoyant piece of cork that keeps bait off the bottom of the flats. When the cork "bobs" beneath the surface, the angler knows a fish has taken the bait.

Circle Hooks

Circle hooks are popular with catch-and-release anglers. These hooks curve back on themselves to create a circle shape. When a fish swallows a piece of bait or a lure, it also swallows the embedded hook. As the fish begins to turn away with its meal, the hook is pulled from the fish's throat. The shape of a circle hook prevents the hook's barb from hooking and puncturing the fish's gills or internal organs. Its shape also causes it to rotate just before leaving the fish's mouth, hooking the fish in the corner of its mouth, a spot where it's easier to remove the hook.

that have one or more metal blades that spin through the water like a propeller. This movement mimics the flash and vibration of live crab or baitfish. A spoon lure is shaped like the bowl of a spoon, which reflects light and can fool some fish into thinking it's a smaller fish and, therefore, food. Crankbaits are hard-bodied lures that may also be called a plug, minnow, or wobbler.

Other Handy Gear

If you are planning to keep the fish you catch so that you can cook them later, you will also need a container to keep the fish fresh and cool. A knife or a pair of scissors can be useful for cutting line. Needle-nosed pliers can come in handy when you're trying to get a hook out of a fish's mouth. You might also want to bring a camera to record your catch, or, if the fish are not biting, to photograph some of the other fascinating aquatic creatures, such as dolphins, manatees, crabs, or water

This angler operates a hemostat (special locking scissors) to remove a hook from a fish's mouth. A pair of needle-nosed pliers is another practical tool used for hook removal.

birds that you might encounter instead. And, of course, don't forget your personal flotation device, sunglasses, and sunscreen.

Specialized Equipment

Flats fishing does not require complicated equipment. However, some anglers like to fish in places that cannot be reached from shore. In these cases, a flat-bottomed boat that can be pushed through the shallows with a pole may be used. Poling the boat through the water instead of using its engine prevents spooking the fish and damaging the fragile ocean bottom. The advantage of using a boat over wading is that you can move from spot to spot looking for fish instead of waiting for the fish to come to you.

Although some anglers hire a fishing guide to take them to known fishing spots, most fish from their own small boats. Fishing from a kayak, for example, may allow an angler to get to places too shallow for other types of boats. Casting from a sitting position may require some practice, though. You'll also need to be able to paddle your kayak

Fishing from a kayak can increase your range, allowing you to explore shallow fishing holes that other types of boats cannot maneuver.

fairly accurately and silently so as not to spook the fish. Landing a fish from a kayak without ending up swimming can be a challenge, but it's often worthwhile if you've found a fishing spot where the competition cannot follow you. You can fish from a single kayak if you are skilled enough to control the boat. A double kayak is a possibility, too. If you are fishing from a double kayak, casting may take some practice so that you don't hook your fishing partner instead of the intended fish. If it is too windy to keep a kayak in place, you can try tying the boat to a tree or other stationary object while you get out and wade.

A global positioning system, or GPS, can be used to help an angler navigate on the water. A GPS unit can be especially helpful if you are trying to find a particular fishing spot that you've been told about or for marking a spot you've successfully fished so that you can find it again in the future. Portable, handheld GPS units are suitable for kayak or canoe fishing. Larger units that can be permanently mounted are available for larger boats, too.

Caring for Your Fishing Equipment

Proper maintenance of fishing tackle is a must if you want it to last. Exposure to salt water can corrode even the most expensive equipment. Sand, shells, and coral also wear down line, lures, and flies. Rinse your gear in fresh water as soon as you return from your fishing trip. Dry it with a cloth, or allow it to completely air-dry before storing it. Inspect, clean, and lubricate (using oil or silicon lubricant for this purpose) all of the moving parts on your reel, and loosen the drag before storing it. In addition, check all of your lines for abrasion or other damage and replace any damaged line to keep it from breaking when you hook your next fish.

CHAPTER 3

UNDERSTANDING FISH AND HOW TO CATCH THEM

Good fishing tackle certainly helps, but if you really want to increase your chances of landing a big fish, you need to know how and why fish behave the way they do. Most fish behavior is driven by one of two things: the need to reproduce or the need to eat while not being eaten.

The Life Cycle of a Fish

Most fish develop from fertilized eggs. Different species have different reproductive strategies, but most flats fish reproduce through a process called broadcast spawning. During this process, female fish release their eggs into open water. At the same time, male fish release sperm. If an egg and sperm meet, the egg may be fertilized. Females

Unlike many flats fish species, which broadcast spawn, the bullhead deposits a cluster of eggs in a nest and guards them from predators.

may release more than a million eggs at a time, but many of these eggs will not be fertilized. Of the ones that are, many will never hatch. Changes in water temperature or oxygen levels, disease, and predators can all prevent a fertilized egg from reaching maturity.

Different fish species spawn at different times of the year. Snook, for example, typically spawn in the summer. Their spawning season begins in April or May and ends around September or October. Bonefish, on the other hand, slow down spawning in the hotter summer months. Peak bonefish spawning season is November through June, although these fish have been known to spawn year-round.

Many flats fish move to deeper water to spawn, where currents can help disperse the developing eggs. Tarpon and bonefish, for example, are believed to travel 100 to 150 miles (161 to 241 km) offshore to spawn. You are unlikely to find these fish on the flats during their peak spawning seasons. Red drum, on the other hand, often spawn in inshore waters near tidal inlets. During spawning, red drum make a characteristic drumming sound that gives the fish their name, possibly to alert other fish to the spawning location. Some fishing lure manufacturers make lures that mimic these sounds as a way to draw fish to the lure.

Depending on the type of fish, the eggs will hatch into small larvae several hours to a few days after fertilization. Red drum eggs, for example, hatch twenty-eight to thirty hours after spawning, while tarpon eggs require two to three days to reach maturity. Bonefish and tarpon have a slightly different life cycle compared to the other flats fish species. When tarpon and bonefish eggs hatch, the larvae don't look like tiny fish. Instead, they are transparent and eel-like. The larvae of these fish live as plankton in the open ocean. After

One interesting point about the snook life cycle is that most male snook transform into females when they reach a certain size.

fourteen to twenty-six days, the larvae that don't get eaten by larger animals undergo a change in shape, or a metamorphosis. After metamorphosis, the juvenile bonefish and tarpon look like smaller versions of the adult fish.

Juvenile fish generally live in freshwater wetlands or shallow saltwater estuaries. These nurseries allow the fish to grow while providing protection from large predators. Adolescent and young adult fish make their way to deeper, more open water as they grow larger.

When fish reach sexual maturity, the fish life cycle begins again with the release of eggs and sperm. Male snook reach sexual maturity in their first year of life. Then somewhere between the ages of one and seven years, males of this species change into females. Therefore, most of the larger snook caught by anglers are mature, breeding females. The one-snook bag limit that Florida has in place is designed to protect this breeding stock.

Fish Food

Knowing what and how fish like to eat can help you decide what kind of bait or lure to use. Knowing what eats them can help you refine your fishing technique. Flats fish come into the intertidal zone to find food. An intertidal zone is the area between low and high tides. Red drum, for example, come into the intertidal zone during high tide to find one of their favorite snacks: fiddler crabs. When the tide goes out, the drum retreat to slightly deeper waters until the tide floods their marshy feeding grounds again.

Snook swim parallel to the shore in the intertidal zone, hunting for minnows and crabs—often in less than a foot of water. Tarpon prefer crab, shrimp, and small baitfish. They can also be scavengers, or bottom-feeders, meaning they will eat dead marine organisms from the bottom of a body of water. When you are trying to catch a

Sight Fishing

Flats fish are easily spooked. The idea behind sight fishing is to see the fish first and then cast to it, preferably with its favorite snack (or something that looks like it) on the end of your hook.

Polarized sunglasses are a necessity for sight fishing. These glasses contain special filters that reduce the glare on the water and allow you to see through it. It's easier to see from the deck of a flats boat. However, if you prefer to wade, try to keep your back to the sun so that you can see. On Florida's west coast, that means casting from the beach in the morning and casting from the water back toward land in the afternoon.

tarpon, live or dead bait or lures that mimic these will work the best. Most other flats fish species also like crab, shrimp, and small fish.

Fish tend to congregate near steep drop-offs and around rocks, stumps, or vegetation because these areas provide cover for smaller fish and other tasty treats. Look for potholes, channel drop-offs, grass clumps, blown-down trees, oyster beds, and rock piles. Channels and cuts through a larger flat area may indicate a fish "highway." These are areas where fish enter or leave a flat as the tides rise and fall. As the tide turns, you may be able to catch traveling fish in these areas.

Fishing Techniques and Tips

A successful angler may scan the flats for signs of fish from the shore or from the elevated position atop a flats boat. Movement of the grass or other vegetation in marshy areas may be a sign that fish are

Casting on the flats without scaring the fish away can take some practice.

present. You may also catch them "tailing." This action means the fish's tail is sticking out of the water as it moves across the flat.

Once you spot a fish, cast about 5 feet (1.5 m) in front of it. Cast any closer and you risk spooking the fish. Most fish are programmed from an early age to be wary of large predators, such as seabirds, and they will flee from anything they perceive as a threat.

If you tend to spook fish on the flats, you may need to practice your casting. You can do so out on the water, or you can make a target that you can cast to in your backyard. To cast a rod with a spin-casting reel, face the area you want your bait or lure to land in and hold down the release button on your reel. Look behind you before you cast to make sure you don't accidentally hook someone. Likewise, look for trees or other obstructions that might snag your hook. When you're sure it's all clear, bend your elbow and raise your hand to move the rod back. When your hand reaches about eye level and the rod is straight up and down, gently move your forearm forward and down. When the tip of the rod comes to about eye level, take your finger off the release button. If your lure lands too close to you, try taking your finger off the release button sooner on your next cast. If the lure goes straight up in the air or lands behind you, you have removed your finger from the release button too soon. Practice until you can get the lure to land where you want it with minimal disturbance to the water.

Remember that fish eat fish or other aquatic animals. They do not expect their food to enter the water from above. If your lure plops into the water in front of them, they are likely to bolt for deeper water. Many anglers attach a leader to their line to avoid spooking fish. A leader is a short section of lighter, thinner line tied to the main line. The thinner line is less visible to the fish, while the main line is still strong enough

You are not the only one out there hunting fish. Shore birds, like this great blue heron, are masters at it. It is well worth watching their techniques.

to pull them in. Be mindful of your shadow on the water because it, too, can cause your prey to beat a hasty retreat.

One of the best ways to learn how to fish the flats is to spend a little time watching shore birds, such as herons and egrets. These wading birds are extremely patient and effective hunters. One of the first things you'll notice about these birds is how slowly they move. Emulating their movements may increase your chances of successfully hooking a fish. Shuffling your feet along the bottom is much quieter than lifting a foot out of the water and plopping it back in. This technique will also help get stingrays and crabs out of your way, whereas a regular step could land your foot directly on top of one of these creatures and increase the risk of injury to you or marine life.

One other fishing technique to practice is called "bowing to the fish." This technique is especially useful when trying to land large, powerful jumpers such as tarpon and bonefish. To "bow" means to thrust the tip of your rod toward the horizon and let it dip to the surface of the water when the fish jumps. This motion reduces the tension on your line and the risk of it snapping and losing the fish.

CHAPTER 4

HANDLING AND KEEPING YOUR CATCH

arpon and bonefish are some of the most prized fish on the flats. These energetic fighters can get quite large and are often a challenge to land. In short, they are a lot of fun to fight. However, they're not generally prized for their flesh. Bonefish, in particular, are catch-and-release only. To ensure the animal's health, it is imperative that anglers planning to fish the flats know how to catch and release a fish appropriately.

Catch-and-Release Techniques

To successfully catch and release a fish, use hooks with barbs that have been filed down or bent back to ensure easy removal. Hook the fish quickly or use a circle hook to prevent the fish from swallowing the hook and accidentally damaging its internal organs or gills. If the fish has

To reduce the stress on the fish, remove the hook with pliers and the least amount of handling that you can manage—and as quickly as possible.

swallowed the hook, cut the line and leave the hook where it is. Trying to remove it will only cause the fish more harm. The acid in the fish's stomach, along with the salt in the water, will eventually dissolve most fishhooks.

Most stores that sell fishing gear also sell dehooking devices, or dehookers. These tools allow an angler to remove a hook quickly without touching the fish, therefore preserving the natural slime coating that protects its skin. Nets can also damage the fish's scales and remove this protective slime, leaving the fish vulnerable to disease. Moreover, never use a gaff. A gaff is a stick with a barbed hook that is sometimes used to land a fish. Stabbing a fish with a gaff will most certainly kill it.

Although flats fish are fun to fight, avoid doing so for long periods of time. The longer a fish jumps and runs trying to get away, the more lactic acid builds up in its body. The stress of a long fight could kill the fish.

Once you have removed the hook, help the fish revive by moving it slowly through the water horizontally as if it were swimming. This motion moves water over the fish's gills and allows it to get the oxygen it needs. If you have been fighting the fish for a long time and it is really tired, reviving it may take a little while. Be patient. You'll be able to feel it when the fish is ready to swim away on its own.

Photographing Your Catch

Just because you have to release a fish doesn't mean you can't come home with a souvenir of your fishing trip. The practice of catching, photographing, and releasing a fish is sometimes referred to as CPR. It is good practice if it is done correctly.

To photograph a fish, hold it horizontally not vertically, especially the larger ones. Fish spend their entire lives in a horizontal position. Their anatomy is well suited for this position, but not for hanging

Be sure that a fish has fully revived from its fight before you release it. If you would like a photograph of your catch, this is a good time to take one.

vertically. Holding a fish vertically by its jaw can damage the jaw structure as well as its internal organs. Even if the fish appears fine and swims away on its own, internal damage may eventually kill it.

Also remember that a fish cannot breathe when it is out of the water. Keep the fish in the water while the camera is being prepared. Once the photographer is ready, pick up your fish with wet hands and hold it horizontally in front of you. Avoid using a towel, rag, or dry hands as you could accidentally harm the fish's skin. Hold the fish with one hand under its belly and the other hand holding its lower jaw. Do not squeeze and never touch the gills. Try holding your breath for the amount of time you have the fish out of water. If during that time you need to take a breath, so does the fish. Put it back in the water as quickly as possible. Another way to get a really good picture is to not remove the fish from the water at all. Instead, have the photographer snap your picture as you release your fish and it swims away.

Keeping Your Catch

Before keeping any fish that you catch, make sure you know the rules and regulations of the area you are fishing in. Obey all size and bag limits. Regardless of bag limits, however, responsible anglers keep only the fish they will eat. This consideration means

Mounting Your Catch

You may have seen fish mounted on a wall in a seafood restaurant or other coastal venue. If the fish is a saltwater species, the mount you see is most likely a replica. These copies are designed to look just like living fish, but they are constructed completely of artificial materials. If you would like to have a trophy mount of a fish you have caught, call around to the taxidermists in your area to find out what fiberglass fish molds they have. It is usually unnecessary to bring the actual fish into the shop. Many taxidermists have standard fish molds for particular lengths of different species. All you need are the measurement of the fish's full body length and a photo. A skilled taxidermist can make a lifelike replica from there. Besides, you can release your catch back into the wild.

you should know what kind of fish you like to eat and what they look like before you go fishing. Be prepared to release any other fish you might catch.

Red drum and snook are the flats fish that most people like to eat. Nevertheless, be aware that you may only keep one redfish if you are fishing in southern Florida and two redfish if you are north of the Tampa Bay area. You're allowed to keep one snook caught on the Atlantic side of Florida, but if you're on the Gulf side, you must release all the snook you catch. Bonefish are catch-and-release only, too. Most people don't eat bonefish anyway. Two tarpon may be kept per person with a special permit. Still, this fish tends to have a strong oily, or "fishy," flavor that some people find distasteful. If you don't like the way it tastes, let it go.

To ensure the continued health of the fish, photograph it while you are holding it horizontally with wet hands and get it back into the water as quickly as possible.

If you're planning to catch and keep fish to eat, it's good to plan ahead. The longer you can keep the fish alive, the better. Many sporting goods stores sell large buckets with aerators in them. An aerator keeps the oxygen level in the water at the correct concentration. In the ocean, carbon dioxide and oxygen are exchanged at the surface of the water. In a bucket, the surface area exposed to the air is smaller and carbon dioxide could build up in the water and kill the fish. The aerator prevents this situation from happening. Another option sold in stores that carry fishing gear is a wire mesh basket designed to float in the water. You tie it to a line and put the fish in the bucket as they are caught. Make sure the basket is completely submerged under

If you are planning to eat some of the fish you catch later, take a cooler of ice with you on your fishing trip.

the water surface. You will also need a cooler full of ice. When you're finished fishing for the day, transfer your catch from the bucket or basket into the cooler for the ride home.

Once you are home, ask an adult to help you clean your catch. To fillet a redfish, lay the fish on its side. Using a sharp knife, make an incision behind the gills down toward the stomach. This cut should go all the way to the backbone, but not through the spine. Now turn the knife horizontally so that its blade points toward the tail. Run the knife along the backbone from just under the gills to the tail. Leave the meat attached at the tail and flip it away from the fish. Now place your knife at the attachment point and, with a slight sawing motion, maneuver the knife between the meat and the skin. Slice the skin away from the meat along the length of the fillet and then remove any rib bones.

When you are ready to cook your catch, you have many options. Redfish has a very mild flavor and it works well with many different herbs, lemon juice, garlic, or other seasonings that you might like. It can be panfried, broiled, or baked.

Some fish carry parasites, however, such as tapeworm and round-worm. To make sure these parasites do not harm humans, all fish should be thoroughly cooked to an internal temperature of 140° Fahrenheit (60° Celsius).

CHAPTER 5

PROTECTING FISH AND THEIR HABITAT

Anglers spend a lot of time on the water, and many feel a responsibility to preserve and protect the fish and fishing grounds that they enjoy. With proper management, fisheries can provide current and future recreational anglers enjoyment for many years to come. Two of the major conservation issues that face the recreational angler are overfishing and pollution.

Overfishing

Although much of the concern about overfishing pertains to commercial fishing operations that pull tons of fish out of the water every day, recreational anglers can and do have an effect on the fish population. Overfishing occurs when so many fish are pulled from the water that there are not enough left behind to breed and replenish the

Species	Minimum Size Limits	Daily Rec. Bag Limit	Remarks
Bonefish		0 per harvester per day	Catch and release only. Hook and line gear only.
Spotted Seatrout	Not less than 15" or more than 20" (statewide) except one fish over 20" per person	5 per harvester per day N.W. Zone 4 per harvester per day S.W. Zone 4 per harvester per day S.E. Zone 6 per harvester per day N.E. Zone	May possess no more than 1 over 20"; included in the regional bag limit. See management zone map.
Tarpon		2 fish possession limit	Requires $50 tarpon tag to possess or harvest. Snatching and spearing prohibited. Boca Grande Pass has seasonal regulations.

Carefully following season restrictions and size and bag limits is not only the law, but also helps keep the fishery healthy and viable for many years to come. The regulations above, for bonefish, spotted seatrout, and tarpon, are based on those provided by the Florida Fish and Wildlife Conservation Commission for basic recreational saltwater fishing in state waters.

stock. This situation not only affects the fish species in question, but also other marine animals that might depend on the overfished species for food. Overfishing a particular species can result in the disruption of the food web and can eventually lead to a collapse of the fishery.

Local authorities combat the threat of overfishing by setting bag and size limits and restricting the capture of certain fish species to particular months of the year. Some fishing guides and recreational anglers also set their personal bag limits lower than what is allowed by fishing regulations. They set them lower because they believe that fish are more valuable to them alive and breeding than they would be as a meal or a trophy. By carefully following size and bag limits, recreational anglers can ensure that there are enough fish of breeding age to support the fishery for the future.

Protecting Bycatch

"Bycatch" is the term used to describe unwanted marine animals that get caught up in commercial fishing nets. These animals, such as sea turtles, dolphins, and juvenile fish, have no commercial value and are usually tossed back into the water. Unfortunately, many of them don't survive their encounter with the nets.

Recreational anglers generally don't produce large bycatch. However, at one time or another, you may accidentally hook an animal you did not intend to, such as a stingray, shark, or seabird. These animals should be immediately and respectfully released

with the minimum amount of stress possible. Stingrays have a barb at the base of their tail, and their stings can be quite painful. Sharks have a mouth full of sharp teeth. Unhooking these animals can be dangerous.

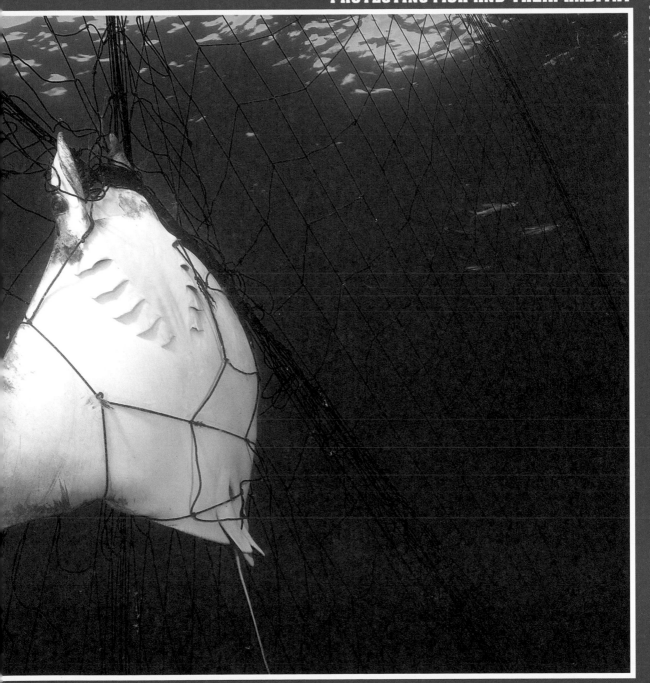

Marine animals such as stingrays, dolphins, and sea turtles that get caught in commercial fishing nets while fishing for other species are called bycatch.

Fishing with hooks with the barbs removed makes it much more likely that the hook will fall out sometime before the animal gets close to you. If the hook does not fall out, however, it's best to have an adult cut the line as close to the hook as possible and let the animal go. Most hooks will eventually rust in the salt water and fall out. Never use stainless-steel hooks; they do not rust. Make sure you leave as little line

Sea Grass

Sea grasses are grasslike flowering plants that live under the surface of the waters of estuaries. These grasses help stabilize the ocean bottom. They also provide a home and hiding place for many marine creatures, including young fish and the animals that fish eat.

One of the largest threats to sea grass is careless boating. Boat propellers can rip sea grass up by the roots, destroying large areas of the estuary that may take decades to recover. When you are on a boat, keep a lookout and avoid shallow water when running at speed. As you are approaching shallow water, slow down and tilt the motor up to avoid contact with the sea grass. If the boat is accidentally run aground, don't try to motor your way out—this action just causes more damage. Instead, use a pole to push your way across the shallows.

attached to the hook as possible. Fishing line is not biodegradable, so it will not break down like the metal hook will.

Fishing hooks and line can kill or permanently injure seabirds. If you accidentally hook a bird, do not cut the line! Take the time to remove the hook. If you are fishing with someone else, ask for his or her assistance. Reel your line in slowly. When the bird is close enough, drape a towel or large cloth over its head to help calm it. When it has calmed, have your friend control the bird's beak by grasping it firmly, but gently. Do not squeeze too tightly or the bird cannot breathe. Fold the bird's wings flat against its body and locate the hook. If the hook still has a barb, push the barb to the outside of the skin and cut it off, then back the hook out. Make sure all fishing line has been removed from the bird and it's uninjured before letting it go. If the bird is injured, or you cannot get the hook out, transport the bird to a local veterinarian or contact your local fish and wildlife agency for assistance.

Pollution Prevention

Water pollution can also endanger fish and their habitats. Excess fertilizer and pesticides find their way into rivers, streams, and estuaries when they are washed into storm drains. Fertilizers are often used to help grass and other plants grow. Pesticides are used to control insects and other pests that eat and destroy vegetation. When they are used properly, these materials generally cause no harm. However, when they are used improperly, they can build up and be washed away, ultimately ending up in the water where they can kill fish or other aquatic organisms.

Another type of water pollution that can be disastrous to fish and marine wildlife is an oil spill. On April 20, 2010, an explosion on an oil well called the *Deepwater Horizon* set off a chain of events that resulted in more than 200 million gallons (757 million liters) of oil being spilled into the Gulf of Mexico. According to an article in the *New York Times* on August 16, 2010, more than seven thousand sea turtles, dolphins, and birds were found dead in the months after the oil spill. Scientists have confirmed that this number is much higher than the normal mortality rate. Commercial and recreational fisheries that were closed after the oil spill reopened a year later on April 19, 2011. The FDA requires any seafood sold to consumers to be tested to make sure it is safe to eat. Research into the long-term effects of the oil spill is ongoing.

Mercury in Fish

Fish are not the only creatures affected by water pollution. Humans may also be harmed if they eat fish caught in polluted waters. The element mercury is one of the contaminants that can be found in fish. Some of the mercury comes from natural sources, such as volcanic eruptions. However, human activity can also result in the release of mercury-containing compounds. Emissions from coal-burning power plants are one of the largest sources of these compounds today. When these emissions settle into the waters of rivers, lakes, and oceans, bacteria can convert the mercury-containing compounds into a form easily absorbed by insects and other small organisms. When small fish eat these organisms, they ingest the mercury-containing compounds, too. Larger fish eat small ones, and the mercury becomes more and more concentrated the higher up the food chain you go.

Overexposure to mercury can cause short-term memory loss, impairment of motor skills, and a higher risk of developing learning disabilities. These effects are most pronounced in the developing brains and nervous systems of unborn babies and young children. For this reason, the U.S. Environmental Protection Agency (EPA) recommends that pregnant women and children under the age of fifteen limit their consumption of fish found to have high mercury content. Red drum and

This angler caught a redfish along the Gulf Coast in Louisiana more than a year after the *Deepwater Horizon* oil spill. Everyone can do his or her part in protecting and cleaning up the environment so that waterways can produce healthy fish for years to come.

snook are considered to be in the moderate risk category. Therefore, it's recommended that pregnant women and children eat no more than one of these fish per month. At the end of 2011, the EPA released a new set of federal regulations that require coal-burning power plants to limit their emissions of several toxic compounds, including those that contain mercury.

You can help preserve your fishing grounds and the fish that live there by avoiding activities that result in water pollution, following all fishing rules and regulations, and conserving energy. Your conservation efforts will decrease the amount of oil and coal needed to make electricity and reward you with a healthier ecosystem. Ensuring that your impact on the environment is minimal can help make certain that your favorite fishery can support your hobby for many years to come.

bag limit The number and size of a particular fish species that each angler is allowed to keep.

biodegradable Capable of being broken down naturally by bacteria or other organisms.

bycatch Animals accidentally caught up in commercial fishing nets.

closed season The months in which catching and keeping a specific fish species is not allowed.

erosion A process by which soil and rock are transported from one spot to another by wind, water, or ice.

estuary An area where freshwater meets saltwater at the mouths of rivers and streams.

fertilizer A substance added to the soil to provide the nutrients that grass and plants need to grow.

fishery The fishing grounds where fish are caught.

flat An area in a body of water that shows little or no change in depth.

float plan Information left with a person onshore that includes information about the boat you are on, the people onboard, when you plan to return, and who to contact if you do not return on time.

fork length The length of a fish measured from the most forward part of its head to the fork in its tail.

habitat The environment in which a plant or animal lives.

inlet A narrow passage between two landmasses.

intertidal zone An area flooded with water during high tide and exposed at low tide.

larva (plural: larvae) The stage of the fish life cycle between hatching and metamorphosis.

metamorphosis The stage of the fish life cycle when it changes from immature to adult form.

open season The months in which catching and keeping a specific fish species is allowed.

personal flotation device (PFD) A device worn to keep you afloat in the water; also called a life preserver, life vest, or life jacket.

pesticide A substance used to control insects or other pests.

pinch-tail criteria The length of a fish measured from the most forward part of its head to the end of its compressed, or pinched, tail.

plankton Tiny animals and plants that float on the surface of the water.

predator An animal that hunts, captures, and eats other animals.

prey An animal that is hunted, captured, and eaten by other animals.

scavenger An animal that eats dead plants or animals.

spawn The release of egg and sperm into the water.

tackle Rods, reels, lures, flies, line, knives, and other fishing equipment.

wetland A swampy, marshy area where the land is saturated with water.

American Sportsfishing Association
1001 North Fairfax Street, Suite 501
Alexandria, VA 22314
(703) 519-9691
Web site: http://asafishing.org
The American Sportsfishing Association works to keep access to fishing
    grounds available for all anglers by acting as the voice for commer-
    cial fishing interests and recreational anglers in talks with
    governmental fisheries management decision makers.

Canadian Sportsfishing Industry Association
1434 Chemong Road, Unit 11
Peterborough, ON K9J 6X2
Canada
(877) 822-8881
Web site: http://www.csia.ca
Like their American counterparts, the Canadian Sportsfishing Industry
    Association acts as the voice for commercial fishing interests and
    recreational anglers in talks with governmental fisheries manage-
    ment decision makers.

Environmental Protection Agency (EPA)
Ariel Rios Building
1200 Pennsylvania Avenue NW
Washington, DC 20460
(202) 272-0167
Web site: http://www.epa.gov
The EPA's website contains a wealth of information about water qual-
    ity, ways to protect estuaries, and many other environmental

topics. They also offer internships for students who are interested in helping to improve air and water quality as well as ensuring protection of these resources for the future.

Fly Fishing Canada
515 Legget Drive, Suite 800
Kanata, ON K2K 3G4
Canada
(613) 599-9600 x208
Web site: http://www.flyfishingcanada.net
Fly Fishing Canada is a nonprofit organization that organizes national and international fly fishing competitions for adults and youths.

International Federation of Fly Fishers
5237 U.S. Highway 89 South, Suite 11
Livingston, MT 59047
(406) 222-9369
Web site: http://www.fedflyfishers.org
The International Federation of Fly Fishers is a nonprofit organization dedicated to the betterment of fly fishing. Its Web site includes educational videos on casting and how to tie flies.

The Nature Conservancy
4245 North Fairfax Drive, Suite 100
Arlington, VA 22203
(703) 841-5300
Web site: http://www.nature.org
The Nature Conservancy is a worldwide organization that funds research and conservation efforts in many habitats, including

freshwater and marine ecosystems. Conservancy scientists have been experimenting with techniques to restore damaged seagrass beds in Florida since 2009.

NOAA Fisheries Service
1315 East West Highway
Silver Spring, MD 20910
(301) 713-2367
Web site: http://www.nmfs.noaa.gov
The National Oceanic and Atmospheric Administration's Fisheries Service is a federal agency that works to preserve sustainable fisheries through research and management.

U.S. Fish and Wildlife Service
1849 C Street NW
Washington, DC 20240
(800) 344-WILD (344-9453)
Web site: http://www.fws.gov
The Fish and Wildlife Service is a federal agency dedicated to the conservation and protection of wildlife and their habitats through research and public education.

Web Sites

Due to the changing nature of Internet links, Rosen Publishing has developed an online list of Web sites related to the subject of this book. This site is updated regularly. Please use this link to access the list:

http://www.rosenlinks.com/FISH/Flats

FoR FuRtHeR ReaDiNg

Anderson, Michael. *Investigating Earth's Oceans*. New York, NY: Rosen
    Publishing, 2011.

Beatty, Richard. *Wetlands*. Chicago, IL: Heinemann-Raintree, 2010.

Carpenter, Tom. *Saltwater Fishing: Snapper, Mackerel, Bluefish, Tuna,
    and More*. Minneapolis, MN: Lerner Publications, 2012.

Crockett, Sally. *Fly Fishing*. New York, NY: Rosen Publishing, 2011.

DeFelice, Cynthia. *The Missing Manatee*. New York, NY: Square
    Fish, 2008.

Feinstein, Stephen. *Conserving and Protecting Water: What You Can
    Do*. Berkeley Heights, NJ: Enslow Publishers, 2010.

Greve, Tom. *Saltwater Fish*. Vero Beach, FL: Rourke Publishing, 2011.

Hynes, Margaret. *Navigators: Oceans and Seas*. New York, NY:
    Kingfisher, 2012.

Jenson-Elliott, Cynthia. *Fly Fishing*. North Mankato, MN: Capstone
    Press, 2011.

Johnson, Jinny. *River and Lake Life*. North Mankato, MN: Smart Apple
    Media, 2011.

Kamberg, Mary-Lane. *Saltwater Fishing*. New York, NY: Rosen
    Publishing, 2011.

Kaye, Cathryn, and Philippe Cousteau. *Going Blue: A Teen Guide to
    Saving Our Oceans, Lakes, Rivers, and Wetlands*. Minneapolis, MN:
    Free Spirit Publishing, 2010.

Keene, Carolyn. *Fishing for Clues* (Nancy Drew: All New Girl Detective
    #26). New York, NY: Aladdin Paperbacks, 2007.

Kurlansky, Mark. *World Without Fish*. New York, NY: Workman
    Publishing Company, 2011.

Larsen, Laurel. *One Night in the Everglades*. Lanham, MD: Taylor Trade
    Publishing, 2012.

Levete, Sarah. *Save the Oceans*. New York, NY: Crabtree
    Publishing, 2011.

Llewellyn, Claire. *Cooking with Meat and Fish*. New York, NY: Rosen Publishing, 2012.

Mason, Paul. *Fishing: The World's Greatest Fishing Spots and Techniques*. North Mankato, MN: Capstone Press, 2011.

Pound, Blake. *Fly Fishing*. Minneapolis, MN: Bellweather Media, 2012.

Schmidt, Pauline. *Let's Go Fishing!: A Book for Beginners*. Lanham, MD: Roberts Rinehart Publishers, 2012.

Stille, Darlene. *The Life Cycle of Fish*. Chicago, IL: Heinemann-Raintree, 2011.

Sundsten, Berndt. *My First Book of Knots*. New York, NY: Skyhorse Publishing, 2009.

Weingarten, E. T. *Fishing*. New York, NY: Gareth Stevens Publishing, 2012.

Wojahn, Rebecca Hogue. *An Estuary Food Chain: A Who-Eats-What Adventure in North America*. Minneapolis, MN: Lerner Publications, 2009.

BIBLIOGRAPHY

Bonefish and Tarpon Trust. "Tarpon Life Cycle." Retrieved September 24, 2012 (http://www.tarbone.org/btt-publications/tarpon-life-cycle.html).

Environmental Protection Agency of Hillsborough County. "Florida Fish Consumption Guide for Mercury." Retrieved October 1, 2012 (http://www.tbep.org/pdfs/fish_rack_card.pdf).

Florida Fish and Wildlife Conservation Commission. "Saltwater Fishing Regulations." Retrieved September 17, 2012 (http://myfwc.com/fishing/saltwater/recreational).

Florida Fish and Wildlife Conservation Commission. "Saltwater Fish Measurement Guidelines." Retrieved September 17, 2012 (http://myfwc.com/fishing/saltwater/recreational/fish-measurement).

Florida Museum of Natural History. "Ichthyology." Retrieved September 29, 2012 (http://www.flmnh.ufl.edu/fish).

Florida Sportsman. "Tarpon at a Glance." August 31, 2011. Retrieved September 28, 2012 (http://www.floridasportsman.com/2011/08/31/sportfish_0007_tarpon_at_a-2).

Maizler, Jan. *Fishing Florida's Flats*. Gainesville, FL: University Press of Florida, 2007.

Mufson, Steven. "Two Years After BP Oil Spill, Offshore Drilling Still Poses Risks." *Washington Post*, April 19, 2012. Retrieved October 1, 2012 (http://www.washingtonpost.com/business/economy/two-years-after-bp-oil-spill-offshore-drilling-still-poses-risks/2012/04/19/gIQAHOkDUT_story.html).

National Commission on the BP *Deepwater Horizon* Oil Spill and Offshore Drilling. "The Gulf Spill." Retrieved September 29, 2012 (http://www.oilspillcommission.gov/media/index.html).

National Weather Service. "Lightning Safety." Retrieved October 1, 2012 (http://www.lightningsafety.noaa.gov/overview.htm).

Park, Haeyoun, G. V. Xaquin, Graham Roberts, Erin Aigner, Shan Carter, and Kevin Quealy. "The Oil Spill's Effects on Wildlife." New York Times, August 16, 2010. Retrieved October 1, 2012 (http://www.nytimes.com/interactive/2010/04/28/us/20100428-spill-map.html).

Sargeant, Frank. *The Redfish Book*. Lakeland, FL: Larson's Outdoor Publishing, 1991.

Sargeant, Frank. *The Snook Book*. Lakeland, FL: Larson's Outdoor Publishing, 1991.

Taylor, Neil. "Catch-and-Release Fish Handling." *Tampa Bay Times*, February 2, 2007. Retrieved September 20, 2012 (http://www.sptimes.com/2007/02/02/Gulfandbay/Catch_and_release_fis.shtml).

University of Florida. "Why Catch and Release?" Retrieved September 21, 2012 (http://catchandrelease.org/overview.shtml).

U.S. Fish and Wildlife Service. "National Survey—2011 Survey." Retrieved September 29, 2012 (http://wsfrprograms.fws.gov/subpages/nationalsurvey/2011_Survey.htm).

INDEX

About the Author

Kristi Lew is the author of more than forty science books for teachers and young people. Fascinated with science from a young age, she studied biochemistry and genetics in college. Before she started writing full-time, Lew worked in genetics laboratories and taught high school science. When she's not writing, she is often out in a kayak on the flats of Tampa Bay searching for tarpon, bonefish, and other Florida wildlife.

About the Consultant

Benjamin Cowan has more than twenty years of both freshwater and saltwater angling experience. In addition to being an avid outdoorsman, Cowan is a member of many conservation organizations. He currently resides in west Tennessee.

Photo Credits

Cover, pp. 1, 3 Jose Azel/Aurora/Getty Images; pp. 4–5, 7, 11, 16, 22, 27, 31, 35, 40, 44, 48 (water) © iStockphoto.com/MichaelJay; pp. 5, 24–25 Jimmy Jacobs; pp. 8, 12, 13, 17, 18, 21, 23, 32, 36, 38–39, 41, 42, 51 Polly Dean; p. 10 Comstock/Thinkstock; p. 28 Kim Taylor © Dorling Kindersley; p. 29 Reinhard Dirscherl/WaterFrame/Getty Images; p. 33 Martin Maritz/Shutterstock.com; pp. 46–47 Brian Skerry/National Geographic Image Collection/Getty Images; back cover and interior silhouettes (figures) © iStockphoto.com/A-Digit, Hemera/Thinkstock; back cover and interior silhouette (grass) © iStockphoto.com/Makhnach_M; back cover silhouette (hook) iStockphoto.com/Jason Derry.

Designer: Brian Garvey; Editor: Kathy Kuhtz Campbell;
Photo Researcher: Marty Levick